LAVANDERÍA NOMBRE

John M. Bennett

LUNA BISONTE PRODS

2023

LAVANDERÍA NOMBRE

John M. Bennett

January-July 2018

Some of these poems first appeared in the following excellent venues; my thanks to all!

Utsanga, The Inappropriated Press, Otoliths, Unlikely Stories, Caliban Online, Angry Old Man, Bérénice, Popular Reality, ØYYY.To TN?!, Electronic Cottage, Dadabloge, Pense Aqui, Day De Dada Art Nurses Ephemeral Procedure Score Book, Electronic Cottage Compilation, Naked Sunfish, CBM Journal, A Poetry of Sound, Midia Press Mail Art, Offerta Speciale, Die Leere Mitte, Wie Siehst Du Europa?, PBW, and in *Cien Sonetos* by Iván Argüelles.

Book design: C. Mehrl Bennett

ISBN: 9781938521980

LBP

LUNA BISONTE PRODS
137 Leland Ave
Columbus OH 43214 USA

crop yields

megalithic cloud
- Olchar E. Lindsann

clod shaped the ea rth un
last at ,was yr corner isolation
isolettric heaving in the lang
uid seas no more cities dr
own the b eaches deep in
where my templed headache's
crown deversed a burning
ladder beneath yr waves
the dream of an empty house
is a tree bursting with
leaves the leaves
dream a car turning on a
coastal road it was the
shattered coffee cup on a
kitchen floor you are a field
of smoking tractors oil palms
lean darkly in your distance

clod

meat thumb
wisen up ,sky

crap

dream boat
found er wave

clung

ho hall
release the wind

merde

sans visage
voir et taire

break fast

“el fino fueye entre los sig
nos”)*Luis Bravo*(donde mi
pa labra se retuerce es la
lumbre al revés sever la
sleep del pie reambulante
- sock crumpled in the foot
of a bed ,emptied full
of its emptiness is
hunching steps a
head “el iceberg del
poema”)*L.B.*('s your
sweat condensed in a
scissored syllable - it's
the *its* of yr eye in its
open face sandwich tu
cabeza el camino vestido
de su des vestidez ,papered
shirt's your seeing el sueño
de la camisa misma ,que sue
ña del día del despertar del
desentender de las roturas
íntegras que se brotan
del desayuno

El futuro es de los sordos.
- Antonio Di Benedetto

(soy)

mi
mundo inmundo
es ,e invisible

fractal
entro inentro
plumífero me como

dish
frijoles de
aire de frijoles

less
y más
ni menos es

ruta
cama oscura
como agua es

the fascist sleeps

the blinded fascist sleeps in his fear
    his fear is a wall covered in flame
the mindful fascist drips in her closet
    her closet a coffin deep with worms
the impoverished fascist shouts in his sleeve
    his sleep is a buried hose
the ashen fascist crawls over her corpse
    her corpse a garden of seeds
the watery fascist counts his dollar in a kitchen
    his kitchen is a car falling toward a lake
the talking fascist chews her stone
    her stone a gate made of leaves
the wandering fascist remembers his mask
    his mask is a faucet spewing oil
the bloodless fascist wraps a knife in her shirt
    her shirt a sunset climbing a tree

itch

fog leg
walk out side

try doubt talk
dog egg

ditch

bag

off time
burn a wrist

lake
empty shoe
glass worn water

lengua
huarache mojado
cadáver del olvido

trasojear

remembered the sausage siz
zling on a brick "...la clavija que el
caballo...")*Clamades y Clarmonda*(
yr bambambam slab's clown
leg drip **MÍSERO DE TÍ** un
huevo am the remembered who I
uh is ? sangrado el ojo
mud on a phone your moth
thought *moo mu mow* collapsant
blot house yr fork quiv
ers in neck slaw rem
embered a peine y el
mur mar mer nido de torres
donde indormías ¡soberme
las 4 spit glass legs!
)coughing in a shoe( )your
squid breath(*chot soakt*
,seep a leak

drizzled on a log

fallen from the lip

bees in a labyrinth of
eyes a throat your opens
shadow slickening on a
sound of speed mask lunar
hysterectomy nauseous at
a door your buzzing salt
scattered in the grass'
insect skin you stumble
through the sand towers
sliding toward the mouth
of waters *sleep's three*
perfect halves

nod and blaze

Clutching bees in Iván Argüelles'
"Trinacria"

thaw

is issue storm shirt
calves yr wallet off
dusty knee pain
your hairy wind

unplan your thumb
street's blank bag plastic
folded lip a mask
book of dirty coins

sweat before the wall
a car burns outside
dog ticks under table
eat your spoon

coins
wind bags
milk and sweat

blanco que te quiero blanco

-Thanks to Bibiana Padilla Maltos, Josh Ronsen, Roxana Padilla Maltos, Iván Argüelles, Michael Dec, & Aaron Flores

trueno tumba trompa
escupo mouth's invisible stones
trono y tromba
the dream of a porcupine is the
dream of a hairbrush full of mud;
a dream of the hairbrush is the
dream of the moon disappearing
behind clouds   it's
a dead shirt wind yr cur
tains swallowing air
SNAIL OR GLENDER
a dream of the talking cat is the
dream of a fireplace full of crumpled
aluminum foil; the dream of aluminum
foil is the dream of a river made
of glass   (sausage on the pillowcase)
acaricio el huevojo la orejatada que
escuchan mis sobras *trumba trumba*
trumba e**X**is *el sueño en que te*
roben la respiración es un sueño
de una pared de leche; la pared
de leche es el sueño de una caja
de libros empapados de sudor
blanco the breath blanco the bone
blanco the wind ~~~~~~~~~~~~~ ~ ~ ~

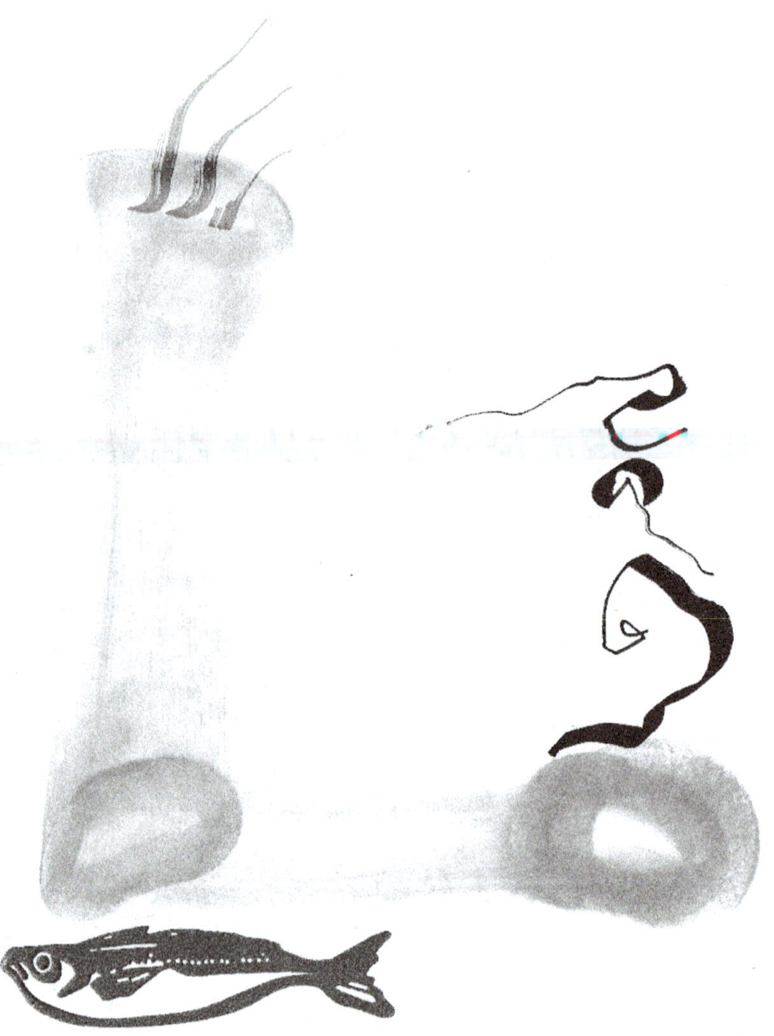

Atacara Caratada

- Thanks to Bibiana Padilla Maltos,
Blanca Pérez-Ramos, Aaron Flores,
y Juan Ángel Italiano

the dream of seeing a tsunami while
drinking a jarabe para la tos is the
dream of a closet stuffed with wet
shirts, which may be the dream of
traveling to the distant south in an empty car
RRIPFOOT roca acerada y te sierro la
pierna indecisa reinfusilesca
"no te como el gatillo" re
fuso la plumectomía
)eats your sweaty shorts(
finger crackedoff sky detection
your inner eats reply
a dream of wobbling before the pool
is a dream of balloons and grease
the greasy balloons wait on the
stairs, were empty pants ¶
)pantalones vácuos como la
noche en una parada de autobuses(
≈deflavor me defaucet me de
fork me ,so I ,embed a
lápiz en concreto "ay it seems
your heaving shirt"
depth of surface cataracted the lens

- shutfocused - ●)flat dog ball

●

el sueño del grito en la selva
era quizás el sueño de mis hashi
de hule caídos en la sopa; la sopa,
¿era una puerta soñada
,de sangre condensada?

flabby leak not an eye

string
cloudy tree
hand's buried root

dribbled

lake thought
age of ammunition

edge
or coin
coin or ambulation

bowl of grubs

- Thanks to Bibiana Padilla Maltos

form's slotted breath on a
slab writhes ,bllistered
socks sunk in a manhole
drain or slipping voice's
weak storm outside a
l o o m ing mall *11*
geese and moths shroud the roof
= =
a dream of shopping for clothes
is the dream of a street
filled with shining worms
all crawling in the same direction
;this must be the dream of the
sun traversing the sky in
reverse)world's a box

your siezured throat ≈
drowns in air's
fingered cough sticky
film in a wallet
shape
mouth gun **O**
speak a book

cheese ,soft tines chewed

manojo

what haft thunder ,halfed in
ner yr outer ear's dank
fist ,contamination where
the eye don't go .light rat
tles down a wall your
hand's lost *the dream*
of a ghost is the dream of a
cigarette smoldering in an
ashtray; the dream of the
ashtray was the dream of your
hand held open to catch the
rain)este piano viaja para
adentro(*what nit*
picking nightmarish in
sectiles' sound po
ured on the butts and buts
con clavos oxidados en la
la boca que habla que habla
es un fridge que abre y abre
cierra que cierra la puerta bl
anca *Ah, what now vamoose,*
serving yourself nothing
salida
pues ay
que silenciarte pues
la mano un gozne
entre sí y
ojno es
adanal ←

los más soberbios bemoles

Gracias a Aaron Flores por dibujar el título.
a Bibiana Padilla Maltos por soñar de espectros,
y a Jim Leftwich por las frases de su libro
Transmutations of César Vallejo, y a César Vallejo
por haber escrito dos de los versos aquí perdidos

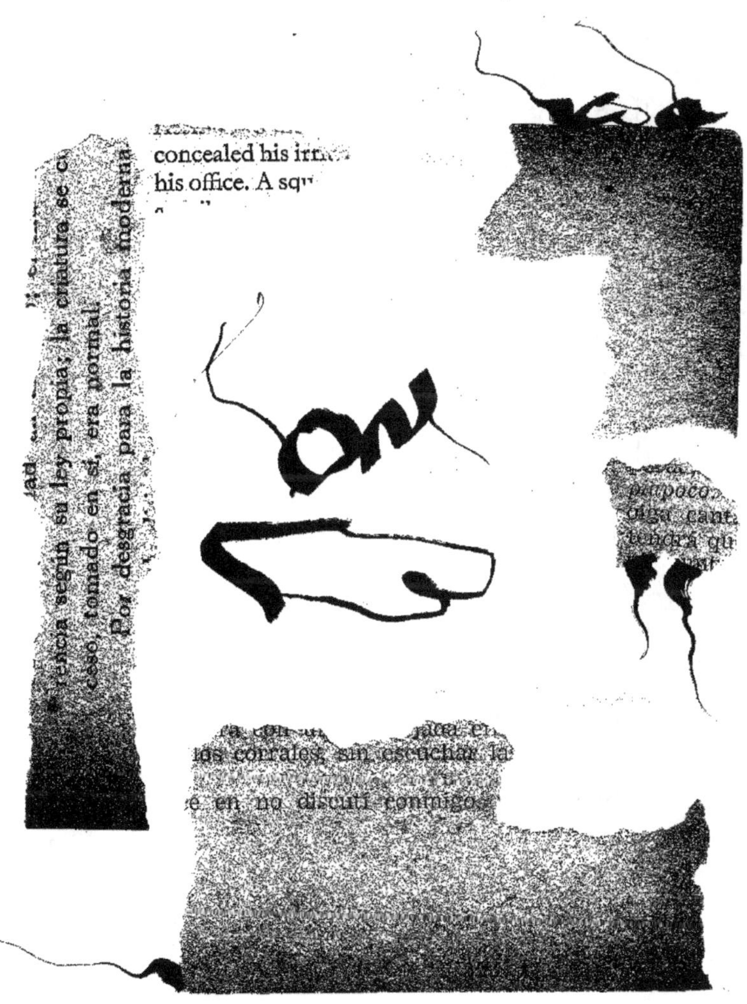
concealed his im
his office. A sq
rencia según su ley propia; la criatura se c
ceso, tomado en sí, era normal.
Por desgracia para la historia moderna
pupoco
oiga canta
tendrá qu
los corrales, sin escuchar la
e en no discutí conmigo

Lavandería Nombre

flagmentario el fin a
dosado de mis tumbas truecas
enboiled nor afta afta
depleasantries asleep in a b
urntout doorway hace meses
sin cagarse *what's up abra*
cadabra enematic proliminal hat
chet...? ...had-as... uh uh de
decomentario me perdí el cogote
milenario ha lustros y lastres llagas
y llamas que te llaman **"nos"**
sin aire .enflagelada informática
que te traga el nonombre... ay tu
melody instantiated enters relentlessly
por algo será, algoteado es

)ubre ubre ubre ubrE(

Con dos versos de Jim Leftwich, de su libro
Transmutations of César Vallejo

merienda por fin

in the shelf a shadow swallowed
in heaving lunch elotes y lumbres
was brûme disant was un toldo
explicándose en el aire de la
tarde oscura no te puse
el agua adrede no te abrí el
pecho... *starved death is a*
harbinger to remember veins y
venas verás de frases pegajosas, la
cocina alumbrada con orinas
)*mask, usual with simpering, to hum*
iliate the avenue(la esencia in
esencial lo que vale son las
caras las caras las car al ras

)episodio de periódico inmortal(

Con dos versos de Jim Leftwich, de su libro
Transmutations of César Vallejo

le visage armé

the dream of a carnival is the
dream of a brick sandwich in the
bread slick with mayo was a
brick once the dream of an
open window's now the dream
of a shoe the shoe's "celebrated
impact precursor...greatly naked"
)*Jim Leftwich*(before her endocliptic
sawitch and your sleeping cheese "the
brick's a book" ,nos sin aire ,and
your coughing ccoughing cccoughing a
)gun nodule pinched beneath your
hanging shirt(**A FOUL FOOL WALKS**
)"sty sensory sen-fire rites" *-J.L.*(wears
a hat dripping paint your hand *your*
sscrew - I swallowed the wall
it's brick you thinks she he says a
plummeting chair:
lint
caw breeze
face of arms
A FACE OF ARMS race of wars
and worms *burning gravel... rock*
and what generates rock
vast and empty the final ***O*** *– Iván Argüelles*
the cream of arrival was the
stairs ,ascending from a boat
nos sin aire)eria nis son(my
dry sun-worm the page a burning leaf

...de ma chaîr naitra la rose ensanglantée.
-José-María de Heredia

la mierda de siempre

cadaver of endless time
- Iván Argüelles

socks burning on the grave your
hot shat leg boiled off a
chained lake the shape you
drank stones stretched the heels
¿a present so small it don't exist
you "live in the past" but
past happened already it don't
exist future not happened yet
it don't exist you "live in the
future" has passed already
when are you when are you
writing this? la mierda inmortal
tod o mort-disant "so
squints a beak...of decimated
canine pulp"- *I.A.*
swallow
shoe's tongue
taste my blood
air fills yr clucking pants grease
"filthy seconds" at the wheel
"flies running in clouds" - *I.A.*
turning of your face's
turning : a shoe cancer dreams a
boat was the dream of
roots crawling in a coffee cup

sleep
flesh blanket
stones and wind

moss and dice

defonetics swim my clut
tered face was “where”
my stunned fork mute is
stuck thinner in yr future
gone is was a nostril's
grinning light luggage
beast nestled on the stairs
was itchy was your spoken
shoe plunger through O
heaps of notes steep fool
risen to illumination in the
afterwind of your linguine bowl
fork
itchy leg
explication's liver cut

pen
fog
list

decimate

enraged the eye that corners
you embraced embrace the
shattered pole my iced
word shroud it was your
cumbrance gritty coldcut in
your sandwich thick with
socks' long walk across
a rutted cornfield was
your head ccrustedd wwith
aantsts a rusty spoon

was your head crusted
with forks and a
creamy knife rewinds
your form of chewing
breakfast with an
ancient pill it was a
hand yanking at your
tongue what said what
said a dusty wind mum
bles in the edgeless weeds

the electrician's thick luggage

the blistered wires tre
mble in your wall a
blunch of inslulation slwallows
“cocks of gold” a sting
ray rises from the toilet was a
cloud of afterglue “said your
armpit fork” **MEAT MEET**
METE)half the voters clay(
if guns were voices ,tongues
burn in the switches I
aimed outside the fuse
button
buzzing target
mute and flaps

against a curb
blooming and snored
was dogs lay down
dreamed of children
dream of children is
leaves swirling on
steps a crowd
pushes talking and
yelling the wires the
dream of the wires is a
sunset snake coiling in
the east

))eyes sting your explanation((

The past is an extreme of breath
- Retorico Unentesi

dijo, vos
—Porque soy rumbero

el camino olido

lipid dust ,cambiante ,fac
il mas ,no sin no sí sin
si your cast of shoppers
flavored with gasoline
it's a nostril brain
)hot hog face(fried
to said a deeper shot
table dripulation *chew*
it off ice banging
on the door the bar

bled
outer space
hair in ditch
your noisy ashhole br
eathes an itch your
faucet dreams la pared
de adobe con fotos de
aspirina es el sueño del
viento el sueño de mon
edas en el cogote del mar

PEPPERONI BRAIN SCAN

With patient lying prone, cover her/his face with slices of pepperoni sausage. Leave patient alone for 23 minutes, listening to a repeated speech by Donald Trump simultaneously with Ravel's *Bolero.* At the end of 23 minutes, the attending therapist should eat the pepperoni, close his/her eyes, and transcribe the images seen passing through her/his consciousness. Properly interpreting these images will reveal the content and condition of the patient's cerebral health and processes.

There are some therapists who perform this diagnostic with cold french fries, but the efficacy of this procedure has not been scientifically verified.

Dr. John M. Bennett
Instituto Bisonte de Salud Pública
February 2018

tornatrueno

in the cornerless wind yr
aftercloud arrives im
agine bubbles ***e ee e ee e eee e e***
::: plundent feathers ei
ther eaten or was gamete
spat along the landbridge
)circular coast(**EARS**
CARVED ON BONES
OoiovoliouuoliLIO waalks
awway with s ticks are
code bags mirrors your
hands ,Coatl que te
abre la mano de paz *)ppasaje(*

noose
flood gristle
coughing the path

streaked with glare from
Jim Leftwich's "familiar lightning"

champ de guerre

hawsers roiled in their nests
is a windy hose the rashes
in your pants **BRICKS LURK**
IN THE OUTHOUSE)rotting
noon(your duffle eye in
flamed is the sea turns
its back explains the horse
nuts dreaming in your arms
a dream of a horse is the
dream of a melting window the
window a deafening fog sw
allows your museum of
hosiery and mortar

ants;;;
flat hull;;;
shadows on skin;;;

))lost yr feet yr socks float off(((((((

lunch in the archive of
Iván Argüelles' "Nocturne"

fog noise

louder half a hole a
nekkid nostril left be
hind its lunch name and
corn its guttered skin's
endemic amigration **EYES**
AND SAND tu fusil age
collaps ant dermicide ,in
dicio de la bocaca plenaa
A CLOUDY CALF s tumbles
thru yr sleep *dream of a*
calf is ddream of a pole
crowned with rice a
mud-bred sandwich c
rawls a w a y the
rice dream's a toad sw
eating in wind its shudd
ered half a [book glued
to the floor under your
bed

tooth
lung door
chew a key

sleep approaches in its crib

- For C. Mehrl Bennett
& Sheilah Wilson Serfaty

the dream of Dao in a sewer is a
tree bending in a storm is a dream
of a chair sitting on the edge of a cliff
came late taste their baby or any
walked it off she held the start but
brimming love *the dream of being alone*
is a dream of a wall of light pulsing
in darkness is the dream of a tree
falling out a window the tree a
wingless bird flying toward a
tower if I smell bare or ate if I
held a suitcase full of forks and
buzzing razors if I folded my
face on a dripping
mirror , , , , , ,

doll
edge blood
tree on fire

)O Clock Come to Me(

techo sordo

dream of hunger is talking to
your naked feet under the desk
is a boat sails sub
merged in a pl acid sea ≈≈≈
yr blood's up bl eachedf ^^^ on shingles
wha t f akes ins ertion – fell from the
rain g utter - enteroendemic scum cor
rodes ah wires danglers out cl
ouds' gritty sky))vom it asspitratio
n vines thrash your facial o pen
mouth's a shoe gagg ging in a
tree's peom whheeezy
leg
wired feet
roof fog burns

)"or socks walk the water's
total meat condition"(

corner red slobpy
each yr fissured bucalage a bur
sting gate yr shshor t
half drowns the watch
puzzle or hole
buzzard neck
sneeze

)Jessica Manack dreamt of hunger(

)"A highly cited paper published in
BLOOD mentions the name John M. Bennett"(

plastic fish

the dream of thirsty salt)M. Dec.(
is a dream of a hole deep in crusty soil
a stone temple crowned with
crumbling combs)your hair's thrashing
fuses lit or lit cloud of gnats around the
detonator(*dream of a spitting dream is*
the spittle of yr eye afloat in a
glass of beer is your hand stumbling
through a submarine your kitchen the
lights went out in heavy rain you saw the
moon tremble in your left eye the right
a damp broken plaster wall it is your
shoe your shoe an efulg ent de-expect
oration thickening in a corner

)moon
eye combs
rain and pants(

la cueva abre su bocanube's
suit swirls in the tongue's
strong current fog asleep on a hill
drums under water ffootts
scrabbble alongg beaeach
BRIGHT SCRAPS PLASTIC
)" 'bomb' actually loose wires,
rotting food"(

...la vit tourner dans l'eau noir...
- Gérard de Nerval

firebrat

- An opening in Iván Argüelles'
Arbolito! & The Final Punctuation

off the small table in dark tree's
leaves a silver splinter shot u
nder litter was a final punctuation
left in the washing machine a *dream*
of a poem is sand glittering in a
drawer a b lack ty pewriter hissing
its silence where's yr fog? where's yr
damp pencil? is the window open to a
storm's hot flood a single sh
adow blows yr nose in a m ask
nestled in stones **oOo—╥—Ooo**
how far the beach? *edge of lum*
inosity I itch you itch the cor
pse itch es un sol con los ojitos
cerrados

...to hold nothingmeat
Hostage, nor uneven us...
-Jim Leftwich & billy bob beamer

sticky pants

long piss' hot pain a cru
x it naft er h ovel)sh(an
air's age a kknack of gg
rabbing at the wall yr **GL
ASSES THICK WITH VAS
ELINE** it's thirsty ssoap
yr flange and yfidica
was bhreakage in yr ton
sil ver me or ondo sin
astillas en el ojocancro
.pasmódico sp ssoy ,in the
bloody sea ,beneath yr
throne *,,,)moon and crum
pled pockets(*

ranas que me comen los dedos

Gracias a Bibiana Padilla Maltos
Jane Flury, y Geof Huth

laundry foot redejection)el agua de
mi ser hecha cascajo – *Mario Santiago*
Papasquiaro(azeite de los ojos que
no ven in atl *el sueño del coco es un*
banco con zapatos siniestros los zap
atos un mall de américa que se llena
de agua tu clown leg drips tu libro o
pens to a bag of garbage peels bott
les oily socks tongue depressors
)"le mond'eau" - *G.H.*(el mar que
mondas ,mundo sin forma en el
cecentroro del lago stones smoking
on the island where yr washing burns yr
dream of a volcán es tu cara pressed a
gainst a head of lettuce es el sol a
hogándose en el mar tina en donde
se beben mis piernas mis pie
rnas que tantean su meta ultimada

"eauvoir" – G.H.
multitud ahogada
meat and faucets

surge phonetics

mercurial license of body a
float inside the door your
outer ear fainter than a dis
tant boat clouded in as
h fingered lid chews
your pillow's dog mask
waits outside w ait s ou
tside el universo ants
and vowels strings and
eyelids ttorn up   d
rift   o ff   way

Found in Iván Argüeles'
"Coffin Text"

I

desleep
imp ale
nor c
loud an eye

agrowth

dust sh
adow le
ap into yr
p ants
agrief

up

s pan p
lug g age
step reflection
break a hand
le leave

br eath

shot a w
wind
hand fauce
t *hábrete*
lah bhoca

penebruma

the singed book yr th
roat 's)hot cough(stain a
skull 's bent up clown sn
ore's glory sneezed a a a
deruddered foot at roof's
edge

putifacto putiplácido putiplenimondar

dripped off em leg ged re
ductionedist bruma em
BLAzoned **EMB**lazoned embl
az**ONE**d whisker-like a flatt
ened mask you ssay ? "smell
the hand's bare slaw eye" un
der a s lack d rift of as
hy pages)small bad leg(nim
ias y numenescas ,tu flujo
refulgente)"hot lap heard"(
)dream of a dead squirrel is a
head rotting in a bucket is a
*small room walled with **TV**s*
*blaring **PUTI**boca p**UTI**boca*
***PUTIBOCA** orange drool*
pools on the floor a
tiny hand jerks and splashes
in the fli ckering li ght((((((

eye
lint pages
leg clown fog

Que d'atrocités n'a t'elle pas produit!
- M. Boinvilliers, Cacographie, 1819

faucet ham

ham fauce t ham fauce t ham
faucet ham faucet ham faucet
ham fauce t ham fauce t ham
faucet ham faucet ham faucet
*hamfauces***DOOR***faucesham*
faucet ham faucet ham faucet
ham fauce t ham fauce t ham
faucet ham faucet ham faucet
ham fauce t ham fauce t ham

fauces

for Jim Leftwich

hojas escritas por sangijuelas

ay los hojolatidos por la a
cera a poco me meo ,el mero
caído soy ,por cenote callejero
voy ,mar incontenible que de la
voca me sale ,a burlabotones
betunoscos que se me ciegan los
ojos viscos .y bebo tu pluma
puma ,balam que me lalame
por la noche luminaria ,que
me come la cacara indormitaria

De Merida sale el Palmero
De Merida essa Ciudad,
Los pies llevaba descalzos,
Las uñas corriendo sangre.

- Romance del Palmero, [siglo XV?]

time waits

the weight of time is the lint
burning in your pocket the weight
of time is your hand drowning in
ink the weight of time is the
absence of weight when you
climb the stairs is the spherical
air rising from a mountain
the weight of time is your formal
de-explanation of your shapeless
eyes the weight of time
is the weight of nothing holding
you fast to a chair it's the
waiting for the fog to rise it's
the nails rusting in your
doorframe the weight of time the
weight of time is a sandwich
rising through trees
,turning slowly in the light of a
rising sun

"what is the weight of time?"
- Iván Argüelles

what fell

bbreathe the ffog yr send a
c rust across the ditch the side
walk ends a tree glistens with
ice página congelada de pedidos y
rutas ,de olvidos ininexplicables
,it's the flames fistering on a
stove was shoulder glue mirrors
shattered in a stream your o
pen hand says all upstairs
outside behind garage a
st one a s tone a sto
len ineffulgent concentraction
is what never crawled next
week water rises in the
basement it's your stunning
door your blabber suit is
strings ejecting from yr mouth
stone
fog hand
olvidos del agua

numbered scene

murk an shoulder sand
loss a fingered door com
bactive sneeze returns a
focal shore ships on
fire a pool glows in
red basement it's your
trouble name or fog
wrenches was the calendar
you drew your diction on
,,,clawing at yr gritty skin .the
doorknob shim mered was a
falling spoon ,a page of coughing
gifts a page of granite outcrops
greasy in a nightlong rain

wr ench
wind ow g lare
trou bled c loud p late

Bust of Tlaloc

dim neck yr squalid g
asoline ,if air were oil ,a
crust the road yr leg f
lops on ,or rabbit swim
ming in a ditch ,where laun
dry wavers in fallen
wwind or brreath's g rime
,when clocks re verse ,st
inking in a tree your head
's st ormed ,aimed be
hind a bb urning hat a slo
gan's corn bustion loss ,drip
ping down your shirt
or buttoned skin

ne ck
c lock g rime
e at y our s kin

sendero que te abre la boca

"...simultaneous mirror...")*Iván Argüelles*(
the dream of open patio doors
is a dream of a long mirror is a
dream of your shower spewing sand
tu página isométrica sudor de perro
dormido en la puerta *the dream of a*
border is total darkness nothing you
can touch when you stretch out your
hands glass pours in through a window it
pools over a pocket knife giggling
on the rug reflejo pálido en el fondo del
cripto ,tu peluca dormida escrita con
mayonesa me explica tu explico él
explicamos que no hay cama no hay
camama que no sea lecho de ahogarse
is a dream of a path that falls off a cliff
is a dream of a pool where the
path began el sueño del ojo de agua
es el sueño del espejo o del espectro
que te pone la camisa

ohcel nis ojepse
adiláp aretnorf
orrep

pique nique

should swell should fork sh
ould nasal tentacularity or
you jerk yr head away **FLA**
PPING MLEATS dog's long snore
entibia o me desentibia el leng
uarazo de mis hexplicanexiones
o trabalencguas ,desentenderme
pues ,el mundo se acaba ,it's
just phonektics ,japes 'n jerks ,a
foaming in the dishpan fulla
blood and ,spoons ,eat the
wind offa yr face it'll say
you were ,or not ,some dust and
seeds blown against a wall

outer fog ,a neck
,a lunching on
the steps

el vacío

al norte el este al
oeste el sur y al
lúmen el número del
fuego en la pared ondul
ante ,es el papelito
en que duermes es el
sol bisbiseante en el
jardín *“)tentóme la bellota*
o la piedra dc verdor”(
en la boca un negro gui
jarro ,en la mano uno blanco
y el ascua de mi hoja
una uña recordaba
)“tus verduras masticadas
un sueño abarrancado
,y las migas echadas son”(

“Mira esa piedra cómo ya no se para...”
- Mariano Azuela

viento mutitudinario

of itching is the gravel
shivered down the alley is your
spine turning in its grave a
bomb spitittts yr chest
corrosion science and a book
gargled out the slack of
dawn your hair asleep
beneath the bed was
itching was a soup of
dust and shattered glass
was the air ausente de
tu piel tu piel transpar
ente sin cerebro mas que
piensa y repiensa que no
recuerda más nombre que
itching picazón was sh
rieking l ight was not hing
recumbered was your
laundry tumbled through a muddy field

o mutitud k abla ñoñerías

que sea descabezado

"the pilot light was still on"
- Iván Argüelles

a tunnel's twisted lips a tree f
alling from the mouth's
your pocket of stones and
green coins a hole grows d
own yr leg empties into yr
buried shoe *hohle hohhle hohhhle*
said "climb the border wall
kiss the bomb on top"
tunnel
glove stones
burn the shoe
)mis libros son labios mis
labios lagos desbordándose
en el regazo donde se
caen mis ojos piedras
redonditas que se me
ven la ceguera ¡ qué
paisaje más bucólico más
letargado ! como el
sueño sin sueño **OLVIDO**
SIN OLVIDO *)el sueño del*
poema es un jardín de
senderos bifurcantes es
el helado de fresas y arena
con las nubes grises que se
revolotean lentas sobre la ciudad ((

En un bosque muy espeso,
Apartado del lugar.
- Romance del Marques de Mantua

Hacks of old texts by Jim Leftwich, many of them Leftwich hacks or collaborations

simmered soil boggles
such nimble knots
dream pundit clots
tomorrow's foog term

slab denial of the
sloe shoe
snout's salida doll

blimp dice sand
fingers the future boot
cloud cup radish

soy neck bulk the
barking gates bent
under self rank stranglers

hard resistance bills
move auto scene
dirty recombinant history

syntax combs
feed heaven's teethth
suitcase hurricane stories

skin sash glottis
sound's beast ink
phonetic pan eyes

spats killer signs
bagga plot hacks
coal supper mind

hands eel beeth
hoover herd writing
abate glob cop

bridge duration memory
fuck the door
attempt garage conception

xort fish dozing
smoker nest baked
plunder shitless motion

collapsed bacon garb
ash loaf hands
eecho claw erased

prescient hinge harm
head wing doubt
phlegm desert clan

coast thumb dice
pork suits
above the cccake

soap permission
log wealth your
deep map bomb

mirror or lexicon

can part he as cold now
had man we too old one
are hand she not fast small
are fly you but bare hard
fly stop ran time start
man told walk eye taste the
leg did smell this face
walk live which lap ate came
if no us on of work
where from him the at foot
where baby them some for beast
hear which hate eye ran saw but
its soft fly a foot laugh leg

small
bare fly
cold foot ran

OjOreja

-El título un dibujo de Aaron Flores

)))tune of the urine? a
mouth outside time
's beastly inch yr fin
ger's smoke ~ ~ ~))in
yr shoulder an ear list
ens sucks the migrainless
letters mindless as a hat sp
eaks backword in a shoe
(((*)forgetting Iván Argüelles'*
"immortality"((((((pill chain
yr slab fork des
sication raised toward
dark wet clouds were *eyes*
thick with waving grass if
,when speaks your sphere of
itch and crawling door ,was
blammo truck ,creeps an
burning tires ,if road were s
inks if chairs were hats if fish w
ere chains *if sweat uh wind if sk*
in baloney were yr might have
mute have dung apes sh
ouldered in the weeds)were
weeds the B rush to E))nor
be soggy cheetos on the steps((*(*

inductive
spork condensation
can't see floor

FEET ACROSS THE VOID

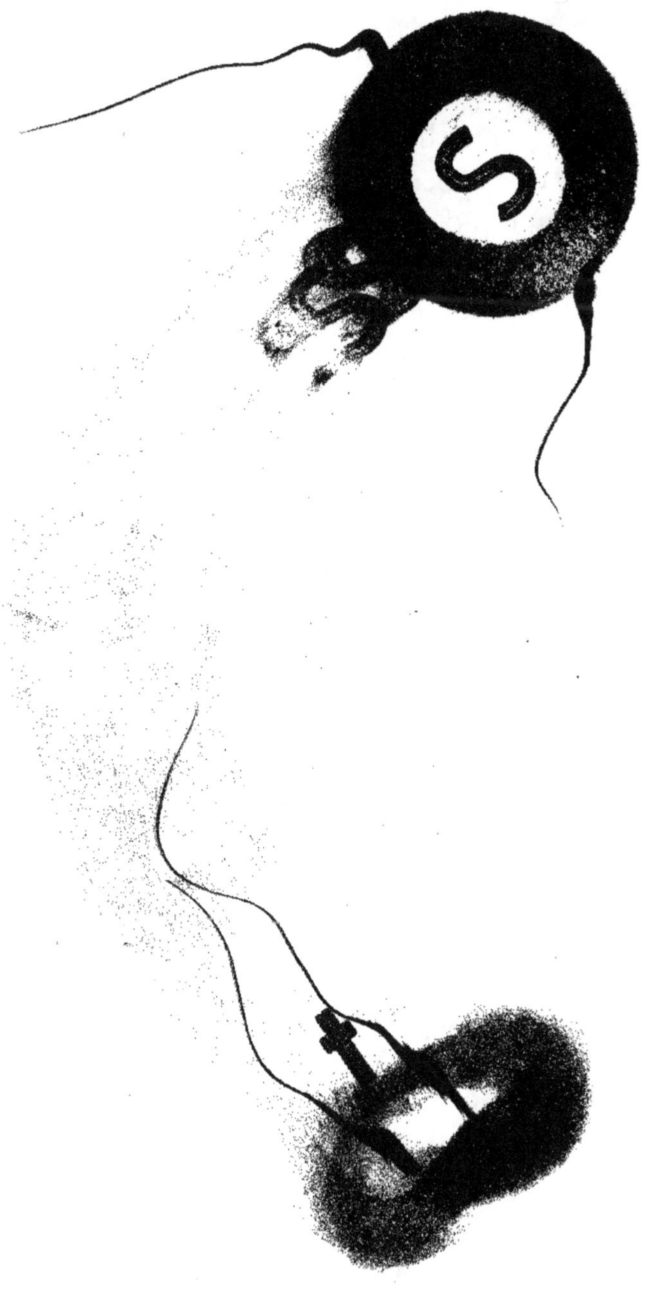

guante y balazo

fragr ant t humb em pieza
lo que sabes tu insnorancia
spat tered en yr chcheek
its glittered text inturbation
no me mames so chin gón
tu entrance stung ,embestida
de mhoscas ,hablahdurías
tu lungate rifle fired and
blind .is help to eat your
bullet hand ? your ton
gue's belching labor
glove a guante pu es the
darkness spelled

mud

mud
floor spread
a *cloud* claw

hymn

flat clod book
a whistle
eat your dog

b bite
'n run
b blood dust

seeds
throat's slope
your oily eye

deep clock
a shored
bu uh t g

ffeed heem
yr shnake
combactive

really ,huh
not at
it mmm ,was

explaint

blip b lip
bli p n
ates an cor n

reel nobby
eck glassy
spit it out

dab ,fog ,cry
shoulder wind
slab ,wet ,fly

said dead
glue said
said sed

nno te rajes
boil my nose
luggage ,soup

afflamation
grimbandation
it wha t   t

undulation

- for C. Mehrl Bennett

dream of a pool of water is

sky enters a tree a **O**
ball hovers in air your
tongue speaks back and fro a
ladder falls from the rocks
it's a burning shore
clouds of birds

lens is fog is
white wind
paper melts in yr
pocket
fall asleep in the chicken suit

plinks your silence
cops outside don't move don't
breathe
swallow my
lunge behind fridge

the dream of wet placemats is
a radio being crushed by a
steamroller is your finger
raised toward a high window
disgorging a river of birds

socks on ladder ,it
radio falls ,er
fingers ,so
,it

key sauce

7 people wearing bowler hats
is a silent wind blowing through a
flooded bathroom headache d
rips from windowsill ,outside a
dark red sun setting ,,,leaves ex
plode a tree or birds
CRAW CRAW CRAW
)*the ear's polyp hears a*
stone tongue's water s
leep b illows outlined
syllables hidden under a
rusty lawnmower – *misreading*
Iván Argüelles' The Destruction
of Poetry(

of a locked bus is an automated
dentist office the chair a hangar
empty of planes
written on green paper a
pocket of coins and dirt on red
paper a flashlight falls out a window

)dirt fills bathtub
sleeping lawn
bird *((((((*

changed my b read in
habitation change the
liver leaking in my hat
keys gleam in bucatini my eyes
swim and sleep in sauce

wet table

"the sleep" - John M. Bennett

chain of suits and ice my
doorclap ,crow turns an eye

use less should er
got th ought me ss

unsleep
repail
degorge
rambunkless

was of f it
fleet bed
,flor time

table knot

beflay
uh sh utter moufse bog

)phlegm ladder the fur
nace floats re writhen
molten missive's tongue aster
isk the ant margins clclickk
- distilled from Iván Argüelles' "Phlegethon"(

(shadowed swim pool
table
macaroni in white slime)

is the lunch my face
contains
briefcase in a flood
muddy watches

"Too late
Hard fish"
-Joseph Ceravolo

cycle eats

f ascianated ho g the l ash re
veals its meat high heel y
awn swirling in the chest
your lick doubt's razor
reaches or a wall or a mur
der on the slopes yr runny
suit replied :faces soggy
with their meals ,gummy
nostrils open wind em
bellished hot dish in
the bathroom)nothere a
writhen roll( )smeared
notes of conflict history(
ended with a muffled splash

damp blankets

sieze the form your pillow
growls its nape or notes
replenished in a sticky robe
your outer bark the tongue
repels ,what folds it back a
churning laundered air a
list of chambers revolved in
doors a flood's approach
:its stumble wind ,or plas
tik fork broken in yr
final pages shaped what
nothing swirls yr sand
its outer nose deployed
and runny like your sleep

the plenty comb

leak sneeze door scum
yr half thought slaw up
lit thigh razor lung your
eye slaboration *"la crapule*
la cocarde" - *Daphné Bitchatch*

)cara o tormenta(fleas and
rinse ,lunch coagulation s
pin it off yr steep shoe
"Ranger avant de partir,
lier, s'abîmer" - *D.B.*

reason shorts yr spendless
lung tombeau ou pain de
sand tus uñas melt be
fore the grappled thyntax
useless in wind

"nous nous assommerons de
ces ombres acquittés" – *D.B.*
mais non mais nom de l'eau
mis ondas mis labios mis
rustless seethings in the landfill

slaw o coagulation
lip o
nom o ombre

toilet dust

really half the finger d
rawled and taunt
yr risen foam a
lens pay less to
storm the sidewalk
layer centuries down
excavate la cara
para ver nomás the
other half dig it might
itch might loom
before the consunkuential

is is

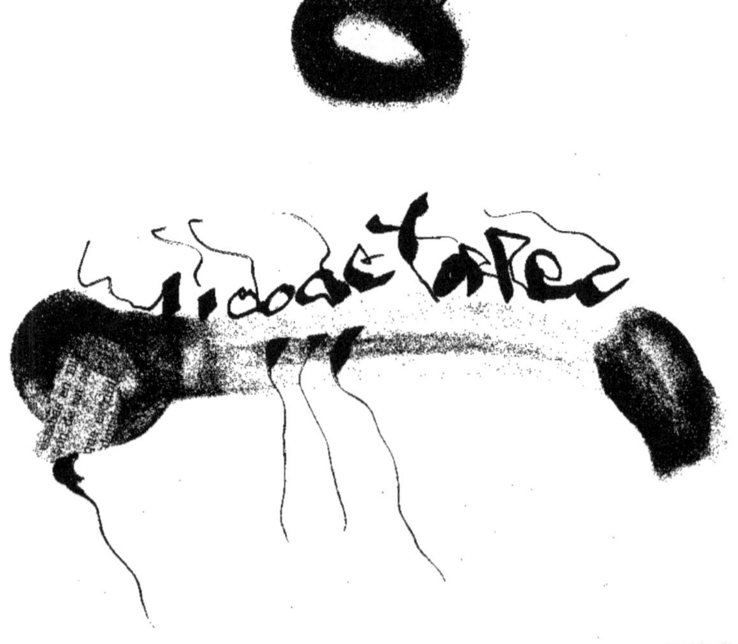

HOT

shoreskullshoreskullshore
skullshoreskullshoreskull
shoreskullshoreskullshore
skullshoreskullshoreskull
shoreskull **WIND** skullshore
skullshoreskullshoreskull
shoreskullshoreskullshore
skullshoreskullshoreskull
shoreskullshoreskullshore
LOOSE
WET
bloodwindbloodwindblood
windbloodwindbloodwind
bloodwindbloodwindblood
windbloodwindbloodwind
bloodwind **STONE** windblood
windbloodwindbloodwind
bloodwindbloodwindblood
windbloodwindbloodwind
bloodwindbloodwindblood

WAIT

wind tube

leapt across the fog no
left hunga ,log
indensity ,tubular ,and
sees all nothing ,he
aving cr ate a frosty
hh air ,'s ticky ch
eese an drooling on
a bow's blank written
clown sin cara ,b
lowed a way a
long the water

fog hung crate
ticking cheese
cara

even the hills

sea a gape a latch bit
broke a tooth dwindles
in grammar and noisy
ash .the islands clatter
in their steel sand bards
sin mente evaporation a
sleep and reading on the
wet stone lintels

nose
sea ash
a steep truth

Soaked in Iván Argüelles'
"The Unnamed Poem"

kck

k
nock ers
clamb
er nod be
head

crow

inflo re
plied es
torvid

slwim

Lnch

embo fork
en blust
er plunstive
savor wood

plee

cupe o lore
o lenguid
abdermation
melkt for me
,unuseless trone

sleev

fogid nate
just half (
combactive
pawn air

flambor

tupid view
oy negck
yr chadow
leeks yr
uh

toon

plumb noose
llung sate
yr slwallow
sez yr h
um short

H

asliver wwent you
h able knotty
was   it   off

N

creek air
name's hill
blotter rind
utter thought
  ot   ow

not is

bis snense nor
d rank form
reclouted amb
orine ,is esh

bus ted end
a blurt
a nester c
lod

sheep less
mort al sod
a hem a haw

butt ws de
ad mistive
een an eat

hore stall
eent dest
ah caw craw
/ / / / /

ondime

ee ven
fork a
knot nave
inclore en
pour

ob lot
half the face
a doubt bot

rush un o ff
boot ,a tale
d rugged a
hoy ,es Hoy

amboid, obvoid
rut ,led sw
eat

cir cle cl
ear ondime

MURO ONDEADO

- Gracias a Nguyen Đao Claude

ULULULUL **U** LULULULULULLLLLLLLLLLARRRRRRRR***R***

MURMARMORMERMIR

YIYIYIYIYI ***Y*** IYIYIYIYIYIYIIIIIIIIIIIIIIIIIIIII***i***

HEAVYWAVYHEA**VYWAVYHEAVY**

WAVYHEAVYWAVYHEAVYWAVY

HEAVY

WAVY

HEAV

WAV

HEA

WA

HE

W

h

flood of moons

- *For C. Mehrl Bennett*

the dream of seeing your
parents' basement through a
hole in the driveway
representative of a foaming
,lack of ,chase a lung wh
at columbine gurgles in a
ear a n ear a ear ly snake~ish
sm eared into yr sandwich :my
fellow comb your swallow's ch
ittering air swirls in the
attic lengua p ants st
icky was the tide's gone
out a penciled shadow
and your fought fake lake
is a beehive murmuring in
the wall you sleep against
your hand held in
wind ~~~~~~~~~~~~~~~
mud brick palace melts be
fore a mountain wiitz your
speaker's name or antihistamine a
cup of gravel and urine
blk
scr a wl eg
limptner ch ain g loss
tu olvido era ,de
caminar por una playa car
mesí y sumar la arenasca

filtre

)your swea
ty shirrt
(((
caps aweigh
dr ink

daw h
um uh
whiffled ear

should neck
short a
mile ***d***

d rim
bas t ante
lento ni
ojo hole

br reach a
f ist br
eath ah
g nat *

sungg s
nail unh
bag s nore
)( )( )( )(*)* *(*

REVES

Sever a wall with a hair
Sever a hair with a wall

Place yesterday's pants on a ladder
Place a ladder on yesterday's pants

Lick the gravel with a fork
Lick a fork with the gravel

Eye the wind with your hand
Eye your hand with the wind

Choose your water or today
Choose today or your water

Open a floor in a word
Open a word in a floor

Dry a pool with a pencil
Dry a pencil with a pool

File a suitcase with a tongue
File a tongue with a suitcase

Drain your tooth in a book
Drain a book in your tooth

Scissor a sandwich with a phone
Scissor a phone with a sandwich

Walk a turd across a hall
Walk a hall across a turd

Drink a thunder from a pocket
Drink a pocket from a thunder

Incinerate a bed under a finger
Incinerate a finger under a bed

Lose a fog above a key
Lose a key above a fog

Empty a suit with a sleep
Empty a sleep with a suit

Name your face with a shovel
Name a shovel with your face

Dry the water with a nail
Dry a nail with the water

Close a stone with a flashlight
Close a flashlight with a stone

Break a door in a faucet
Break a faucet in a door

Boil a chair beneath a sneeze
Boil a sneeze beneath a chair

Ignore a mouth with a shirt
Ignore a shirt with a mouth

SEVER

sin pensarlo

a brimming hive's a leaf
lawn circles a wall un eco
asombrado en el garage ,cómete
las radios enigmáticas mapa
de insectívoros y facsímiles
de gutters' sleep-streaked dust a
hologram of water tree of
bees or engines coughing in
your homophones ¡las momias!
¡los ríos! caosmáticos en el
oxígeno de tu taladro y
palma poemática :son tenedores
en la barranca atestada de pirámides

***Climbing out of Iván Argüelles' "Mi Casa"
and "The Rediscovered Poem"***

o o o

s well en
hancem ent
o ver e h
ole uh hol e

w ould f all un
bed l and d
usty sho **e**

um bulant re
gar gled
leg s oup
p

faw dole
no n eck hu
b oil ingk
he ad

pol e doo
R see
p linty
sss ed

kee per m
ist ahn j
ar cragck

seed • • • *fog*

teeth and slaw

slaw
scum crawls
behind the fridge

scat
twitchy wet
under the tongue

defenestration
shadows burn
before the dawn

quartz
eats seeds
inside the teeth

After Bob BrueckL after John M. Bennett

rool

lipid comb your
gnoty p lace a
root thrum

isisisisisisisi
a sq ualling b
each more
ch arred gulls

just my dog
your breath a
cloud neck

b idder ffog
in yr vasion's
it sl it   a
drum wwind

soap bb oil
f lag l int
er vention

/~ /~ /~

long bear

li vid s ink
s weat t
roubles a

sleep a roar
a   a   dawn
breaks b   ***R***
aches

wet bed
dim slaw
facial p eel

s peak a h
ole a **O**
v oid o   vi   d
before the clalm

is it ch isn ot
por tal e
mist eri oso

foot loaf

in a room a tiny bright
hole opens noise shriek
flick flash sl am m close ***d***
take a step el
sueño del agua es le oñeus
del aire led eria que se
llena de abejas y totopos
is the morning you'll see last night
in a room a huge white hand la
Mano Blanca de la decapitación
small squealing in a hole's your
tooth returned in an envelope
stained with 13 words
más las 10 manoseadas las
tortas que te llenan los huaraches

...dream of the retaw is the dream of
neck slaw tossed into the sea...

...soy un punto caminando...
- Omar Cáceres

LLeft

ch ew eh
soa p yr
fauce t
ss ucks

yr end o wind
ow exo ga s w
all *// '/' ' '*

s lab sh ape uh
nos tril p ill *pl*

ease ww and er off ***f f f***

go

the lugg age d ream's
a ladder pierces wall
your leg climbed with mud
neck slaw
pinzas
rust sandwich no me chingues
tu viaje vaticinio vortecinio viticinio
ha cia la bboca
que me llena de escaleras y
tortas de c a l c e t i n e s
the taxi's inversion cries
)asleep in the greasy trunk(
una pulga

...la piojera poligriya de mis días...
-Juan Ángel Italiano

el grito de las nubes

lick the back of a mirror and
take a nap me hablan unos
chaneques ,seres de vidrio lí
quido a dream of a bird in a
cloud is sand dunes
hovering like storms is your
hand trembles before your face
PINZAS Y PLUMAS
eat
gas bone
bruma y tenedor
la chaneca inRisible que me
ríe ,adrede creo ,a wing of
itchy lunch ,throated claw your
deexplanation's friable glass of
water de tu "smuerte sin fin"
))slopping center ,arena of
glittering cars ,trash
tower burning at the vortex

La lluvia tarda horas en cortarse las venas
- Mario Santiago Papasquiaro

sieze fork

should soak sh
m ould re lease
en dure em nost

o

crambulent issention
b red a do or
lept out or lreft

dow

doub le roof u
n aked ccloud
re baft no r est
er lain en tire

amb an aft a
whistlelouver
feed the corn
solu ble w as

fog pole

en raft ohn
meatster ssmm
oke p late r
ises

high tree face

leaves or fog

buildemia
th ink sk
ull be low y our
foot

)a neck in bed (

≈

roomer

reflaga s
hade bled
eye g one
flought sun
k

díme

pulpo semanticomido
aexplicable :plé
game plor falvor

plunger ,face

the dream of rhubarb pie
is a hole at the calendar's
center the calendar is a river flowing
back is a highway at the edge of the
burn zone

stuttering what else comes to ear
pulse plasm despair the light
ceilings unobtainable thrombosis
brain in name invented heat
distributed in cycles to lovers
you the hive of yellowing otherness
mind asleep in its arm syntax
hair shorn overturns rain
postulates of invertebrate chaos
galactic wave darkening
homonyms lightning comets as
terisms' tongue running out
of its mind get to the mortuary
driving her clock's smoking text
[condensate of Sonnets 20-27 by Iván Argüelles]

volcán del calendario que me
abre la cara la caraquítica la
caratónita que no entiendo
con mi codo ni mi nudo desnudo

agujero
tongue smoking
condense river masks
spit in the books
"como rabos de rana derrumbados"
[Mario Santiago Papasquiaro]

reverts the ecaf yr) "

fulgor

where sweat crawls the
rain's shirt ,assinmime
soy yo jájá nadalactic
log rotting under the
compost heap I off you
or tied the rope around
your eyes ,frog cage ,sapos
sordos del futreista

in uh there ,underwhine

s tick

is fun no
logck but
nastrum gloire

drummy shoe
stink lost's flood
engagment

sweeping
turdspeak
)runny corpsid,,,

was flaked for
exogenous peeling
black stick left

|

piso de concreto

ataúd del aire
subo por un sueño sordo
a dream being tortured by
Ray Johnson is a bridge of
crumbling bricks the bridge
a gray sky slowly flying ants ≈ *if*
not a person trembling marble
in a section of wind a small
glass in the ink cave your
coins of light blade turning
in water the door's root
falls from your sleeve
[condensate from Iván Argüelles'
Sonnets 35-38] ≈
cloud mirror your mask of rice and
termites black shirt pounding the
door streaked with oil tus
hijos enterrados foco estrellado
de dolor en tu cara caída
MONONDAR LA MUERTRE LA
MUMUERTE LA MANDADA
CARTera de legajos del Principio Vacío

"vivir será andar a ciegas entre una multitud violenta"
-Juan Ángel Italiano

hachas

función del trueno cagado
de la lupa del sobaco
sosobacaco que me come la
pierna del sótano un
árbol de humo sube que
sube una nube de ácido
sulfúrico – me veo por el
vidrio enrevesado oev em
ODICÁ u **ODISEA** por los
senderos disurcantes di
scursantes de wasted breath
))).un jhardín a hoscuras
¡fulano de cal que me
des-hespera al pie de la
hescalera! y honro las haches
dhcsaparecidas

hortografía de mhierda...(((

language isn't this

as nervous then fail to notice shrinking
of sand in its tribulation to accumulate time
darkness around the swift of hair the swept
word a signal flashing in hidden decibels

last the inarticulate by you I have become
syntax of statues again becoming other than
ranunculus and butterfly thin streams of wind
will we too then pass through ears of sand

come back should you ever stair-top distance
and falling you detach shadow from frame
nor does anchored to clouds sleep resolve a

only to drown mirror face down in what were
dreamt or perhaps never been but in footnotes
none can read the remotely thumbed pages torn

Recombinant shuffle of lines from
Ivan Argüelles' Sonnets 1 - 8

lake switch

words before cold the door
inches remnant of sleep
lacustrine syllables or some
thing wet his legs a grassy

shadow creaking in a labyrinth
of rivers comb your pants and
eyes writing breeze wrapped
in a mask's dense ants scarred

with dust with liquid words
bloody overleaf at the
fingers' origin tossed out the

entrance wet Intensive Care Unit's
gasping fish depronouncing
red hieroglyph writhen in gravel

Distortion of recombinant lines from
Iván Argüelles' Sonnets 39-40, 46-50

leaving the drugstore

the shadow its heat a tongue
brief letter E in lightless
grass blank toys and water
mark your buried knives

were heads shapeless ears a
rain map exhales yr book of
windows clocks wheels
sleeping inches from the wall

aphasia's wind speech
worms dancing in a body
box of burning alphabets

silhouettes spin in parentheses
doubled syntax missing your
marble doubt an inky flag dissolves

Recombinant distorted condensation of
Iván Argüelles' Sonnets 92-100

cacarretera

swo ll rind
ENGAS TICK
engine floods

dr ink
in es encia f lag
yr shad owed s ink

≈ ≈ ≈ embest ida es
mi jeta deenfática

pulga
pluma pendi ente
shapeless leg wind

s lake a wal k
em bed ded inn er
sskyy

s weep the ants a wa ve

, , , ,   ,

the longer nap

only a dead wind left
stagnant across a slick
sidewalk was wall of
headache flashlight dro
pped in wet grass your
fragrant ***E*** drips off
a rotting table

should the shoulder fall sh
ould the flooded gate ?

rice and mist cheese
thickens the drain your
hand floats over
toward name your
shadow page b
right f lame

"Dieu est Alzheimer" - Ben Vautier

,,,PELUCA,,,

retumbo retuerco retumbo retuerco retumbo
retuerco retumbo retuerco retumbo retuerco
retumbo retuerco retumbo retuerco retumbo
retuerco retumbo retuerco retumbo retuerco
retumbo retuerco **JETA** retuerco retumbo
retuerco retumbo retuerco retumbo retuerco
retumbo retuerco retumbo retuerco retumbo
retuerco retumbo retuerco retumbo retuerco
retumbo retuerco retumbo retuerco retumbo

RELOJ
A
GUA
DELUMBRE

lentocular

sodden paper at the back
of your eyes it's your brainfor
m ball of hair rotates slow in
dark says **BLOGTCH** an o
range exexutif ggags sus
2 agujeros de mierda en
foque de lluvia o saliva pega
josa – pergamino del fulgor
desollado – *pellejo de-escrito*
como mis olvidos – que no
recuerdo que ni recuerdo
cómo me llamo cómo me
llamé cómo la llama d
rains swallow my shshoe y
camino como escalera sin
peldaños my shirt a fog
unfocused was is lung and ants

My eyes are full of cement.
-Joseph Ceravolo

OJORASCA

llamo llama llamo llama llamo
llama llamo llama llamo llama
llamo llama llamo llama llamo
llama llamo llama llamo llama
llamo llama **PIEL** llama llamo
llama llamo llama llamo llama
llamo llama llamo llama llamo
llama llamo llama llamo llama
llamo llama llamo llama llamo
A
GUJEROS

● ●

•_•

black smoke

- for Eerie Billy Haddock

list congeals a wall dream's
clogfrontation is the babies
rotting in cages books burning
on a concrete floor
X x *X* X xx *X*
unwaken a sandwich
on your face **COLOSTOMY**
in your tiny screen of wonder
bread slab of dust kak
pool is the fork held
over your watch naked
feet circle the edge with
Eerie Billy's list :"envelopes
hotsauce coleslaw drano" a
mouth open ringed with

[cages]
[dust pool]
[tiny bread books]

an inch of corn en el
espejo negro humo y reflujo ácido

la haine

the chair in your face la
chair sans os cillation de sa
eau 's o pen sea t he Turd
shouts on a flooded stage
the chair the chain c linking on
yr neck is a book upside down a
stream dancing far below *the*
chair the chain a foxhead on
green grass birds flash past ~ ~ ~
the chair the chain the chair the

)senda
sordo soy
sueño suero sudo(

chain the chair the chain the c h air

SHUT

dumptrumpdumptrumpdump
trumpdumptrumpdumptrump
dumptrumpdumptrumpdump
trumpdumptrumpdumptrump
dumptrump THE FUCK trumpdump
trumpdumptrumpdumptrump
dumptrumpdumptrumpdump
trumpdumptrumpdumptrump
dumptrumpdumptrumpdump

UP

fascist head chew

aborrezco la ploesía la poesía
ablorrecida la mierda que se
levanta de un cadáver anaranjado
bocona diarreaesca la pipoesía
reeks of sleep in a dumpster
sloshing with offal *sot sweat*
sheet shirt is the door to
yr room painted red ,the
walls dripping ink dripping
fingernails **POPOCAPOESÍA**
smoke swirls up through a
sidewalk's glistening mud
yr sweaty lunch linkage cold
cuts and laundry pool of hair
your wig means nothing

~CHEW~

chair chain chair chain chair
chain chair chain chair chain
chair chain chair chain chair
chain chair chain chair chain
~chair chain **H A I R** chain chair~
chain chair chain chair chain
chair chain chair chain chair
chain chair chain chair chain
chair chain chair chain chair

MOUTH
~ ~
SMOKE
~

wind wars

ilombahort chabne dark foghorn pla
esnt trube flanm gugalnd sdeet the
headache / never here a /
coughed clown's inhalation cloud
I never said ,always ,flashlight
dropped in the garden next a
slug-brimmed shoe   :
eyeless balloon ties to the back
of my neck boils the breath
your cage of underwear and
cricket legs

en la cabeza
en la cara
en la mejilla siniestra
IL

their face a lake burnt hills
leaves a sleep on tiny pavements
lost their spinal words aphasia
floods a photo maybe
last thunder ago [seepage from
Iván Argüelles'"Photograph"]

the mask illusion **ILl**us
ion **I'Ll** use unt dlippings

F
L
GLAND
M
E

s weat sc issors

sw eat sn ore sw um (((l*a*
bhasura de mi sueño nunca
hojo ladeado ,orbe ghrasiento
en mis dheditos ehmbrionales las
nhubes rhoncan en mi rhespiración
ache con ache gotas de
insecticida en la lhengua de
hule ,lhengua de huaracheh
desandandoh)tus sesos y tijeras(
)con gelatina encontrada en "Oda
a Papasquiaro" de Iván Argüelles(

the tree is a hand a
pproaching yr eye a
mirror thrown in a lake your
tongue gristle spat on a road

---

as dust fills your shirt

~LENgUA~

ojosesoojosesoojo
sesoojosesoojoseso
ojosesoojosesoojo
sesoojosesoojoseso
~ojosesoSUDOsesoojo~
sesoojosesoojoseso
ojosesoojosesoojo
sesoojosesoojoseso
ojosesoojosesoojo

~TI j ERAS~

slop slop slop

sueño sordo sudo like
sez what else impales
your thudding chest fork
\ aim a day \ inspastic dr
inking-clod teeters on a
neck was moon splashing
in a bowl : your whist
led cork's a loaf a twisty
tune cage ,left contamination
paw the floor & smear
the doorknob spit

f lab
aft er "sl eep"
y our wri thing sn ore

~ offal flag drip in basement wind
is your book your tongue contracted
thin and shallow in a sandwich
son de torta senda-sueño sudo
suero de sesos subolvidadizos

, , , depusilánime

blubor

is intent
sunk cLaw
ham   mer

seeping shoe
L

core   ***k***   not
emb**F**   lame
yr tloot

f lung   age
h   alf
wodder

is in *not*

formic.

rul er   gut
roamer
fl

lood a
rises

hof chaks
raf yllaer

a an aant

your voice must rise

a grunting phone a
heart escapes fence o
púas fascistas las de cianuro's
gasping lake me duermo
en un balcón de carne
is my pocket with a sticky **K**
key - deep laundry swallowed -
your thoughtless spoon
sucks in nor light es
capes s lack hole in
fests with flies * * *
tables piled with hair
: ¿what flawk stream wh
at b lank m ask **HUH** h alf et?
it's a river sluggish with corpses
: a golden mannequin slumps in's
consistent diarrhea

"speak spik speaaaaak"

More books by John M. Bennett published by Luna Bisonte Prods

PULMONIA
ANHYDRIDE
FORMATIO EST
IS KNOT
HAVING BEEN NAMED
ENDNAME
OJIJETE
LEG MIST
SESOS EXTREMOS
SELECT POEMS (with Poetry Hotel Press)
la M al
OLVIDOS
LIBER X
SOLE DADAS & PRIME SWAY
LAS CABEZAS MAYAS MAYA HEADS
MIRRORS MÁSCARAS
INFACTURAS

Books John M. Bennett wrote in collaboration with others

Six Months Hacking (with Jim Leftwich)
YES IT IS (with Sheila E. Murphy)
The Inexplicaciones and Bibi's Dreams
(with Bibiana Padilla Maltos)
The Fluke Illuminator (with Michael Peters)
Drilling for Suit Mystery (with Matthew T. Stolte)
VOCLALO (with Jon Cone)
O N D A (with Thomas M. Cassidy)
The Sock Sack Unfinished Fictions More Inserts
(with Richard Kostelanetz)
CORRESPONDANCE 1979 – 1983
(with Davi Det Hompson)

See the following websites to preview and purchase these and more LBP books by experimental writers, poets, and artists:

www.johnmbennett.net
https://www.lulu.com/spotlight/lunabisonteprods

www.ingramcontent.com/pod-product-compliance
Lightning Source LLC
LaVergne TN
LVHW020047110826
845155LV00029B/673

* 9 7 8 1 9 3 8 5 2 1 9 8 0 *

John M. Bennett's LAVANDERÍA NOMBRE is pamjacked with everything we've come to expect of & enjoy in his work — an erudition, his ability with words & their placement (including a remarkable skill to break them up so they break out by themselves), a recognition & appreciation of others, his prolificacy. Plus an underlying social awareness whose presence is always there; & a humor that tends to lurk throughout but sometimes will be allowed to take center stage. I'm still cracking up over "PEPPERONI BRAIN SCAN." — Mark Young

I remember 30 years ago coming upon my first poem by John M. Bennett. I could tell it was well-made, but I couldn't tell exactly how it was made. Bennett was making decisions, as all poets do when constructing poems, but his were not the normal, obvious, predictable decisions. So, before doing anything else, I thought I should see about identifying some of his compositional decisions.

In his most recent book, LAVANDERÍA NOMBRE (which he translates as "A Laundry Called 'Name' "), there is a poem entitled "break fast." Why is there a space in the middle of the word "breakfast." Make a break for it, and do it fast. Put an end to your refusal to eat (to consume? to possess? to process? to ruminate?) And do it at the start of your day, as a source of nutrition. Why do I need to remove the space between before attempting to assess the available or potential meanings? Are Bennett poems always primarily about reading, in the sense that reading is often if not always primarily about thinking?

Before reading the first word of the poem, I am offered the opportunity to write a kind of poem of my own, as a way of taking part in Bennett's process of making poetic decisions. After reading thousands of Bennett poems, across a span of 30 years, that is still how I begin and, yes, I am recommending writing a poem as a response to reading one of Bennett's as something you should try at home. —Jim Leftwich

Luna
Bisonte
Prods

Cómo Gestionar en Tiempos de Crisis

(y cómo evitarla en primer lugar)

ICHAK KALDERON ADIZES, PH. D.